Would You Believe...

in 1500, platform shoes were outlawed?

and other **fashion** follies

Richard Platt

Contents

OXFORD
UNIVERSITY PRESS

Great Clarendon Street, Oxford OX2 6DP

Oxford University Press is a department of the University of Oxford. It furthers the University's objective of excellence in research, scholarship, and education by publishing worldwide in

Oxford   New York

Auckland   Cape Town   Dar es Salaam   Hong Kong
Karachi   Kuala Lumpur   Madrid   Melbourne
Mexico City   Nairobi   New Delhi   Shanghai
Taipei   Toronto

With offices in

Argentina   Austria   Brazil   Chile   Czech Republic
France   Greece   Guatemala   Hungary   Italy   Japan
Poland   Portugal   Singapore   South Korea   Switzerland
Thailand   Turkey   Ukraine   Vietnam

Oxford is a registered trade mark of Oxford University Press in the UK and in certain other countries

British Library Cataloguing in Publication Data

Data available

ISBN-13: 978-0-19-911502-0

1 3 5 7 9 10 8 6 4 2

Originated by Oxford University Press

Created by BOOKWORK Ltd

Printed in China by Imago

WARNING: *The practices in this book are for information only and should not be tried at home!*

Introduction

WHAT ARE YOU WEARING today? Are you a slave to fashion, buying catwalk styles as soon as they make it to the high street? Maybe you go your own way, mixing and matching individual clothes to create a look that's entirely original. Or do you shun fashion altogether, and just wear black?

However outrageous your style, you'll have trouble matching the most extreme fashions from the past, or from around the world. Are you into piercings? How about wearing a plate the size of a saucer in your lip? Or if high heels are your thing, maybe you'd like to totter around on the 75-cm (30-in) monsters popular in 16th century Venice?

In this book, you can read about these fashions, and many more that you won't want to imitate. If some sound appealing, be wary of copying them. A waist you can wrap your hands around might turn a few heads, but you'd have to risk breaking some ribs to achieve it!

Would You Believe...?

When, where, who, which, what? When was there a fine for wearing fur? Whereabouts in the world did 600 women use makeup to kill their husbands? Who made the first bras? Which women had the tiniest waists? What fabric was worth more than gold? If you want to find out the answers, read on!

Fashionable
Figures

STARING DOWN from billboards or gazing from glossy magazines, fashion models are sometimes hard to tell apart. Always tall, thin and tanned, they challenge us to lose weight so we can squeeze into ever smaller clothes. But it wasn't always like this. Ancient people had very different ideas of beauty.

For Stone-Age folk, fat was fantastic! The statues they created show bulging bodies. In a world where food was scarce – and there was a risk that tonight's dinner might bite its hunters – being thin meant being sick or weak.

▲ **Stone-Age good looks**
Created about 6,000 years ago, this fist-sized pottery figure shows that Stone-Age artists admired shapely women who could provide many healthy babies. The "sleeping lady" came from the cave temple of Hal Saflieni, discovered in 1902 on the Mediterranean island of Malta.

Studying paintings at an art gallery, or leafing through a vintage magazine to look at the photographs, shows that the obsession with being thin is surprisingly new.

Artists like 16th-century Flemish painter Rubens show women as plump, happy and attractive

Hourglass

In the 1950s, the perfect figure was an "8" – not a size eight, but a small waist between a bulgy bottom and top. Thin meant fashionable only from the 1980s. Stick-like thinness is unhealthy, though: the truly trendy balance good looks with sensible eating.

Fuller film star ▶
American movie star Jayne Mansfield showed that plump was glamorous. She wowed movie audiences in the mid-1950s with her generous figure.

▲ **Skinny chic**
Fashion photos for designer Calvin Klein made English model Kate Mos famous in the 1990s. Her extreme thinness made it fashionable to loc like a waif (a starved young girl.) Women have to endure permanen hunger and risk potentially dangerous diets to achieve this loc

Ancient
World

SWELTERING IN the dusty desert heat of the Nile Valley, women in ancient Egypt had a hard time looking smart. To keep their draped see-through linen dresses beautifully crisp and clean, wealthy Egyptians swapped them as often as four times a day.

Rich and poor

Egyptian fashions changed slowly, but women and men showed off their wealth and style with collars, bangles and belts of gold and precious stone. Poorer folk wore simpler jewellery made of colourful pottery beads.

▼ **Perfume cones**
In Egyptian paintings men and women are often shown wearing "perfume cones" on their wigs. But nobody has ever found one: artists may have drawn the shape to show that the wig was scented.

In ancient Greece and Rome, getting dressed meant winding yourself in lengths of fabric. Pins and weights held them in place. Styles rarely changed, but fashionable women did not dare to wear last season's colours.

▼ Ancient Rome
The *stola* worn by Roman women was made from cotton, silk or wool. It covered the whole body and, in public, respectable women covered their heads, too. One Roman citizen, Sulpicius Gallus, even divorced his wife because she left the house with her head uncovered.

Most Egyptian men wore pleated skirts

◄ Ancient Greece
Ancient Greek men and women dressed in garments called *chitons*: long lengths of fabric draped over the shoulders and tied around the waist. This statue from the 4th century BCE shows a woman wearing a cloak called a *himation* over her *chiton*.

Would You Believe...?

Costly clothing
Purple silk was the ultimate fashion fabric in ancient Rome. Silk was imported all the way from distant Asia, and was worth its weight in gold. The purple used to dye it was 20 times more costly. It was made from sea snails: 10,000 of them made enough dye to colour one garment.

One Roman fabric was made to look like clotted blood – it was black, but sparkled in sunlight

▲ Roman rules
The Romans started sumptuary
laws in 215 BC to control
extravagant spending. The first
rule banned women from
wearing gold jewellery weighing
more than 14 grams (0.5 oz).
This golden bracelet would
have been banned.

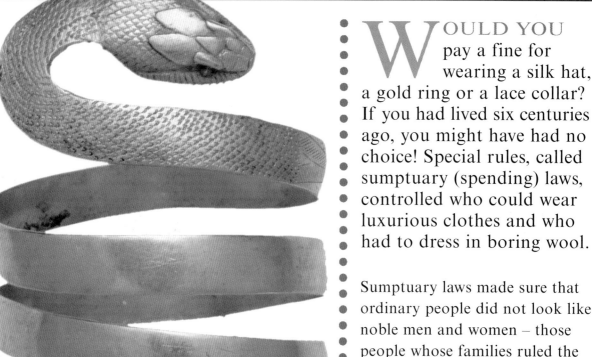

WOULD YOU
pay a fine for
wearing a silk hat,
a gold ring or a lace collar?
If you had lived six centuries
ago, you might have had no
choice! Special rules, called
sumptuary (spending) laws,
controlled who could wear
luxurious clothes and who
had to dress in boring wool.

Sumptuary laws made sure that
ordinary people did not look like
noble men and women – those
people whose families ruled the
land. The laws also aimed to limit
the amount of costly goods brought
in from abroad, because buying
them harmed the nation's trade.

Peasantly fashionable ▶
The poor people who grew
crops to feed their rich, well-
dressed masters had to wear
woollen clothes, either undyed
or in dull shades. English farm
workers wore traditional
clothes in these colours until
the early 20th century.

Knights and merchants

King Edward III ruled in 1337 that nobody less important than a knight could wear fur (he later let merchants wear it – if they were five times richer than knights!). Sumptuary laws soon ended, but they set styles for working people's clothes until just a century ago.

Would You Believe...?

Breaking the rules

People who broke sumptuary laws usually just had to pay a fine. But under a 15th-century Mexican law, those who dressed too smartly faced a far stiffer penalty. Moctezuma I, emperor of the ruling Aztecs, ordered the execution of anyone wearing jewellery grander than was allowed.

In the 17th century, foreign lace was completely banned in France

▲ **Jewels and gems**
Bans on buttons seem strange now, but in the 14th century buttons were often carved from precious stones. These Chinese buttons are made of jade, which only nobles were allowed to wear.

Coronation costumes ▶
The clothes worn by England's royal family on special occasions are rich in materials once controlled by sumptuary laws. This crowning dress has a trim of ermine fur, which nobody below a lord could wear.

GARB BANS

FLORENCE, 1322
Silk and scarlet clothes can only be worn in the home.

ENGLAND, 1362
Yeomen and below cannot wear silk, silver, chains, jewels or buttons.

PERUGIA, ITALY, 1366
Velvet, silk and satin are banned.

FRANCE, 1583
Only princes can wear jewels and pearls on their clothes; gold and silver embroidery are banned.

CHINA, 1680s
Yellow clothes are banned for all except the emperor's friends and family.

Smooth
Operator

◄ **Roman tweezers**
A visit to the public baths was a painful experience for rich Roman men and women. They screamed as their slaves plucked out their armpit hairs, using tools like the tweezers on the right of this set.

B Y SHAVING, scraping, waxing or plucking, women since ancient times have tried to make their skin as smooth and hairless as polished marble. Most men shared their pain, cutting their chins daily with blades of stone or bronze.

In ancient China, dancers desperate for smooth skin once removed hair with *rhusma* – burning quicklime mixed with poisonous arsenic. Later generations played safe with painful pumice or tweezers.

▲ **Shaving stone**
Pumice stone, thrown out by erupting volcanoes, was one of the first razors. Its rough surface can be used to scrape off hair. English writer Samuel Pepys recorded in his diary for May 25th, 1662, that pumice shaved him "easily, speedily and cleanly".

Sugar solution ▶
Sugaring is a way to get rid of hair, first used in ancient Egypt and still popular today. A sticky solution of sugar, lemon juice and water is pressed on to the skin, then stripped away – removing the hair at the root.

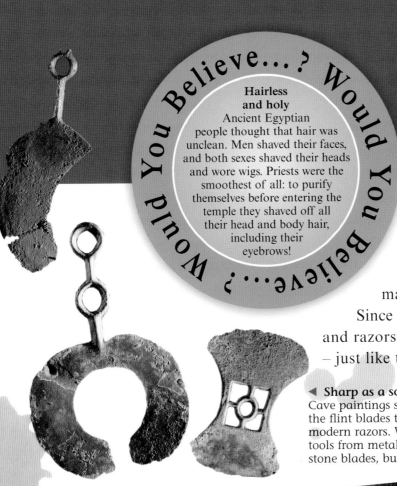

Would You Believe...?

Hairless and holy
Ancient Egyptian people thought that hair was unclean. Men shaved their faces, and both sexes shaved their heads and wore wigs. Priests were the smoothest of all: to purify themselves before entering the temple they shaved off all their head and body hair, including their eyebrows!

In 1915, advertisements first featured women with shaved armpits. The lie that hair was unhealthy made smooth skin fashionable. Since then, sales of waxes, creams and razors have never stopped growing – just like the hair they briefly remove.

◄ Sharp as a scalpel
Cave paintings show Stone-Age men without beards: the flint blades they shaved with were as sharp as modern razors. When men learned how to make tools from metal, bronze razors like these replaced stone blades, but they were not as sharp.

◄ Sunday shave
Until "safety razors" were invented in 1762, men shaved using sharp, straight blades. These were called "cut-throat" razors because, used carelessly, they could do exactly that. Many men preferred to trust the work of shaving to a barber rather than risk wounding themselves, as this humorous picture makes clear.

Fashion
Victims

CHECKING THE MIRROR, a fashion victim primps and pouts, adjusts a feather or two, then steps out – on to the battlefield. It isn't just catwalk queens who follow fashion: when soldiers from the past went to war they literally dressed to kill!

● ● ● ● ● ● ● ● ● ● ● ● ● ● ● ● ● ● ●

Practical yet stylish
Until the 17th century, European soldiers wore whatever they liked, but this made it hard to tell friend from foe in chaotic battles. Uniforms made a target of anyone in clothes that didn't match your own.

▲ French fashions
Medieval knights spent freely on fashions: styles in armour changed quickly, and a new steel suit cost as much as a car does today. Parade armour was the most elaborate. Never intended for battle, it was decorated with brilliant colours, gold and silver.

Samurai armour ▶
Japanese noblemen called samurai fought from the 12th to the 19th century in armour made of beautifully varnished metal and bamboo. They fixed coloured flags to their backs to identify themselves on the battlefield. Some wore elaborate helmets decorated with paper and leather nearly a metre (3 ft) high or wide.

The red coats of British soldiers made them stand out clearly in the sights of their foe's rifles

17th-century European officers used their uniforms to show off their wealth, adding rich embroidery, feathers and gold. Armies became a glittering mass of colour. This fashion parade ended in about 1890, when new uniforms in drab colours made soldiers harder to spot and shoot.

◀ **Emperor's finery**
Soldiers' uniforms were at their colourful best at the start of the 19th century. French emperor Napoleon, shown here, looked magnificent in gold buttons and trimmings. Even ordinary cavalry uniforms were made by the best Paris tailors and cost the equivalent of £1,500.

If You've Got it, Flaunt it

HOW LOW CAN YOU GO? When it comes to necklines, nobody went lower than the ancient Greeks. They worshipped women who wore tops that completely exposed their breasts. Ever since, women have tussled with "tut-tutters" in a battle over what it is decent to reveal.

It's not just the bust that causes a stir. Catwalk fashion models hide nothing, but even a glimpse of a woman's ankle can be shocking to some people. What you show is less important than where and when you show it. What's decent on the beach will raise eyebrows in a shopping centre!

● ● ● ● ● ● ● ● ● ● ● ●

◀ **Bare-breasted fashion**
Minoan women from the Mediterranean island of Crete may have worn costumes that showed off their shapely breasts. This picture is based on a pottery figure made 3,600 years ago for a religious ceremony. Minoan women were men's equals, and even took part in sports such as boxing and bull-leaping.

14

The careful 50s ▶
Screen heroine Marilyn Monroe reveals almost all that was respectable on the beach in the 1950s. Yet just ten years after this picture was taken, American fashion designer Rudi Gernreich introduced the first topless swimsuits. They caused outrage, but topless dresses followed not long after.

Miniskirts got shorter **in the 1960s as women's liberation moved on: by 1967, they** barely covered the bottom

Keeping it covered ▶
For much of the 19th century, Western women's fashions covered the whole body, often concealing even the neck and ankles. Although exposed flesh was considered shocking, the same was not true of a woman's shape. Figure-hugging dresses showed off women's curves.

Miss Beehive

BIG HAIR BEGAN IN ANCIENT ROME. Wealthy women employed an *ornatrix* to arrange their hair into high, wobbling piles. Women's hair did not reach the same heights again until the 18th century. Then topknots towered so high that they sometimes touched candles hung from the ceiling, and caught fire!

▲ **High-rise hair**
The huge hair creations of the 18th century were constructed on high frames. Besides false hair, they sometimes included flowers, feathers or even model ships. The sculptures were expected to last three weeks before they needed rebuilding.

Geisha hair ▶
Perfect hair was essential for Japan's geisha girls (traditional artist-entertainers). Starting in the 17th century, they combed up their hair into a style called *shimada*. The shiny black hair contrasted brilliantly with the geishas' white face makeup.

The beehive ▼
This high-piled style was named after dome-shaped beehives made from coiled rope. The aerosol hairspray that made it possible was invented in 1948. Made from varnish, the spray left the hair hard and sticky, and it was impossible to wash out.

Big hair was back in fashion in the 1950s, thanks to the invention of hairspray, which held tall styles in place. Men used greasy creams to sculpt "quiffs" that rolled over their foreheads like breaking waves. Big hair came back again in the 1980s, when styling gel made possible towering "Mohicans" and punky spikes in lurid colours.

Would You Believe...?

Horns of hair
Princesses of Tibet wore their hair sculpted into wide horns. Their maids wound their hair around light wooden sticks that stuck out 40 cm (14 in) on either side of their heads. The head-dresses stayed in place all the time, and stopped the princesses from turning their heads while asleep.

A Hat for all Occasions

IF HATS DID NOTHING but keep off the sun and rain, most of us would only rarely need them. But hats do much more than this. They can tell the world who we are; how rich, fashionable or important we are; and whether we are working or playing.

Hats pass on these messages because they are hard to miss when someone looks at us. And wearing the same hat as a big group of people suggests that we are all in the same club or clan.

The more beautiful the ladies, the higher were the steeples on their heads

▲ **High hats**
French and German women's hats reached a towering peak in the 15th century with a style called the "henin" or "steeple". The veil that hung from the tip sometimes fell to the waist. When it became fashionable for these giant hats to hide all the hair, women plucked or shaved their foreheads.

▲ **Tricorne hat**
Men had worn hats with the brim cocked (turned up) in earlier times, but in the 18th century it became fashionable to cock three sides, creating a three-cornered or "tricorne" hat. The hats were for carrying and posing only – they soon fell off their owners' huge wigs.

Poor beaver
In the 17th century, the best material for making men's felt hats was beaver fur. This was so scarce that a good beaver hat cost a labourer four month's wages and a maid one year's wages. Nations fought wars for the best beaver land, and trapping made beavers almost extinct in Europe.

Would You Believe...

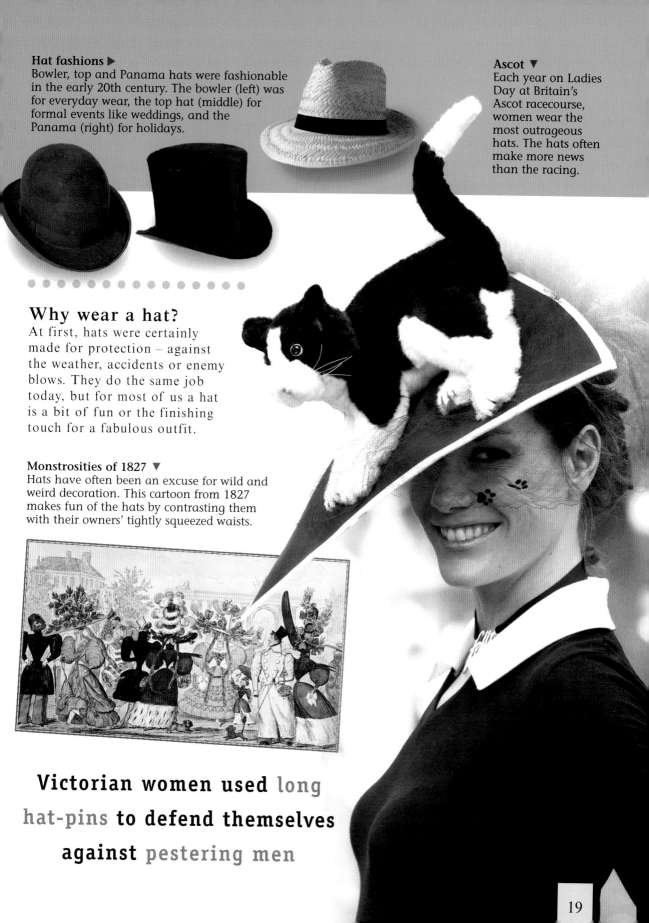

Hat fashions ▶
Bowler, top and Panama hats were fashionable in the early 20th century. The bowler (left) was for everyday wear, the top hat (middle) for formal events like weddings, and the Panama (right) for holidays.

Ascot ▼
Each year on Ladies Day at Britain's Ascot racecourse, women wear the most outrageous hats. The hats often make more news than the racing.

Why wear a hat?

At first, hats were certainly made for protection – against the weather, accidents or enemy blows. They do the same job today, but for most of us a hat is a bit of fun or the finishing touch for a fabulous outfit.

Monstrosities of 1827 ▼
Hats have often been an excuse for wild and weird decoration. This cartoon from 1827 makes fun of the hats by contrasting them with their owners' tightly squeezed waists.

Victorian women used long hat-pins to defend themselves against pestering men

Wild and
Untamed

IN THE LONG GRASS OF ITS south Asian homelands, the tiger's stripes are a perfect camouflage. They make this elegant and powerful cat almost invisible. On the back of a wealthy woman, a tiger skin does the opposite, making her stand out as cruel, selfish and caring nothing for the natural world.

Dressing in "exotic" furs, feathers and ivory used to be the fashionable way of showing off wealth and status. Now it's a crime, because hunting threatens to wipe out some of the world's most rare and beautiful animals. A century ago, there were probably 100,000 tigers. Fewer than 5,000 survive today.

● ● ● ● ● ● ● ● ● ● ● ●

Fur coat ▶
Since humans first hunted, they have valued fur for its warmth, softness and beauty. In 1954, when this picture was taken, there seemed nothing wrong with wearing a coat made of leopard skins. The growth of the environmental ("green") movement in the 1970s changed people's views.

▲ Pet trade
Furriers (tailors who make clothes from fur) can legally use cat and dog skins in Europe (but not in the USA). Some animal welfare organisations believe the trade in pet fur is cruel, and are campaigning to stop it.

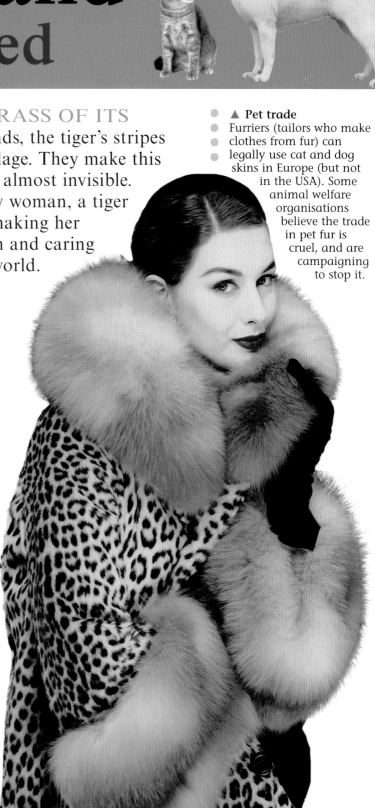

In 2004, Tibetan customs officers **found the skins of 31 tigers and 581 leopards in a single lorry**

Illegal trade

Since 1975, the Convention on International Trade in Endangered Species (CITES) has banned the sale of skins and other parts of endangered animals.

▼ Big cats

The beautiful skin of the big cats makes them the most prized of all fur animals. They are at risk not only because of hunting, but also because the growth of cities, roads and farms means they have fewer places to live.

Tiger (South and East Asia)

Ocelot (South and Central America)

Jaguar (South and Central America)

◄ Prized plumes

The colourful feathers of birds of paradise once decorated hats. Hunting the birds stopped when it became clear that they were endangered. But today they are threatened once again, as loggers clear their forest homes in New Guinea.

Anti-fur protests

For some animal lovers, CITES does not go far enough. They believe farming animals for their skin is cruel. Their noisy protests have stopped many fashion designers from using real fur.

▲ Faking it

Nobody need wear real fur or skins. Manufacturers can create convincing look-alike materials with artificial fibres. However, furriers point out that real fur from farmed animals is "greener". Unlike fun fur, it rots when thrown away, and comes from a renewable source.

21

Bras and Bindings

BIG BUSTS OR SMALL? Fashion decides the shape, but it's a brassiere that provides it. Simple bras began in ancient Greece, with the *apodesme* – a rolled strip of cloth that lifted and supported the breasts. Roman women hid their breasts, binding them in a soft leather *mamilare*.

● ● ● ● ● ● ● ● ● ● ● ● ● ● ● ● ● ●

The modern brassiere started out in the UK under the name "bust girdle", sold by the Jaeger fashion house in 1904. It was given its modern name seven years later in the USA.

Would You Believe...?

Cantilevered bra

When Jane Russell was filming *The Outlaw*, the film's millionaire director Howard Hughes was unhappy with her costume. A keen pilot, he used aviation technology to design a special seamless bra with extra support. Unknown to Hughes, Russell never wore it because it was too uncomfortable.

Cones on top ▶

Madonna put her bra centre stage on her 1990 "Blond Ambition" tour, flaunting it as a fashion garment and inspiring millions of imitations. Designed by Jean-Paul Gaultier, the cone-shaped cups copied and exaggerated the fashions of the 1950s, turning underwear into outer-wear. As planned, Madonna's outfit and act caused outrage, and the Pope called for people to boycott her show.

Fashion in bras alternates between the Greek and Roman shapes, either flaunting or hiding the breasts. Today, bras are the most complicated of all garments: some are made by hand from more than 20 pieces of fabric.

▼ Push-up revolution

Underwear that makes the cleavage look bigger is nothing new – it was popular in the 18th century. But the modern version is a lot more comfortable. Stretch fabrics and padding provide support, and new microfibre fabrics give bras a super-soft feel.

Busts swell **when business booms:** flat chests **are fashionable in hard times**

Crinolines
and Bustles

▲ 18th-century paniers (meaning "bread baskets") were worn to spread dresses width-ways.

I N A DRESS THE SIZE of a small tent, how would you get through a door or sit on a chair? Wealthy women in the 16th century had to find ways to do these things because, beneath their skirts, they wore hooped frames called farthingales to spread out the fabric.

Wealthy 16th-century women lived leisurely lives but, when the fashion for hooped dresses returned with crinolines in 1850, women of all classes wore them.

◄ **Farthingales**
The fashion for farthingales came from 15th-century Spain, where dressmakers used rope, woven grass, willow or whale bone to stiffen skirts. By the early 1600s, fashionable women were lifting and spreading their skirts with hoops the shape and size of cartwheels.

Beastly bustles ►
Victorian women padded out the backs of their skirts with huge and ridiculous devices called bustles. Some bustles were so wide and flat people joked that you could safely stand a tray of tea-cups on them.

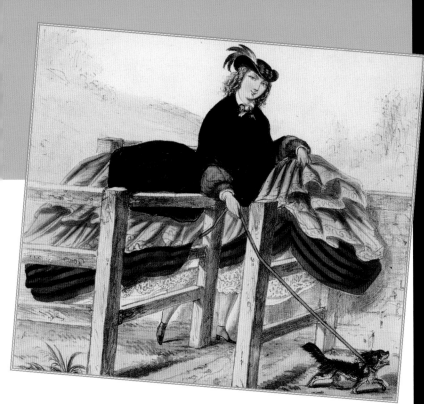

▲ Crinolines
This humorous print shows just one of the problems that crinolines caused. Hoops of springy steel made going through doors and gates possible. But, as crinolines billowed to 180 cm (6 feet) across, women who tripped over could not even get up without help.

● ●

In factories, swirling crinolines caught in machines; in fields, mud and rain clung to farm girls' impractical hooped skirts. The fashion didn't last long: within 20 years, the crinoline had given way to the bustle, which exaggerated the shape and size of womens' bottoms. To this day, bustles and hoops are still worn to fill out fancy wedding dresses.

Would You Believe...? Would You Believe...?

Special chairs
Crinolines changed the shape, not only of the women who wore them, but of furniture, too. Sitting in a crinoline was tricky: all too often the front sprang up. Special chairs with short legs and a sloping back left extra space for the yards of spreading fabric, and solved the problem.

Farthingales were the most inconvenient and uncomfortable garments in history

Scaling down
Bustles changed from the 1860s, when they began to replace crinolines, through to their disappearance by 1890.

Construction ▲
Bustles started as "bum-rolls" – cushions tied above the hips to make a dress look fuller. Sprung steel hoops were introduced to make bustles lighter, but the smaller, later bustles got their fullness from layers of pleated fabric.

YOU CAN'T BREATHE. YOU CAN'T walk. You can't sit down. A tightly-laced corset may make your waist look tiny, but wearing one can be torture. Corsets are toughened, stiffened underwear. They are designed to squeeze the body into fashionable, often unnatural, shapes.

Invented 4,000 years ago in ancient Greece, corsets went to the extreme at the end of the 19th century, when the fashion was for figures that resembled an hourglass or a wasp.

▲ Child-sized
Children's bones are soft and bendy, so adults believed that the younger they put their daughters in corsets, the less harm it would do. Underwear manufacturers usually recommended child-sized corsets, not for their slimming effect, but as a way of keeping a child's back straight.

◄ Menswear
Men wore corsets to slim their waists and padding to emphasise other parts, as shown in this 1819 cartoon. The two servants dressing this "dandy" (fashionable man) are pulling on the laces that tighten his corset.

Not just for ladies
Beneath their starched shirts, some 19th-century men wore corsets to flatten their bulging stomachs. British prime minister Benjamin Disraeli wore one, and rivals of American president Martin van Buren claimed that he did, too.

Would You Believe...? Would You Believe...? Would

Fatal contraction
Corsets affected the health of millions, and occasionally even killed those who wore them. In 1859, a French woman died three days after going to a ball sporting a very narrow waist. An examination of her body showed that her corset had snapped three ribs, forcing them into her liver.

Risky business

Men's corsets were not as tight as women's, which crushed the ribs so hard that it was difficult to breathe. Fashionable women ignored doctors' advice and, starved of oxygen, the slightest exercise made them faint.

◄ **Whale of a time**
Fabric was not stiff enough to squeeze the waist, so corset makers used stiffeners made from whale bone. "Boning" gives this corset a 48-cm (19-in) waist. Rubber-covered steel replaced bone in 1912.

19th-century brides aimed to have a waist no larger in inches than their age – and most got married before they were 21

▲ **Squeeze me**
Tight corsets squeezed the body so much that the internal organs moved around – the liver was sometimes almost split. Besides shortness of breath, corsets also caused constipation and indigestion.

Squeezing and Shaping

▼ **Cradleboards**
Native Americans carried their children tied to cradleboards like this one. The board flattened the back of the skull. People in the Northwest went further, using boards that also pressed the child's forehead. The peaked shape this produced was a sign of beauty.

YOU'RE NEVER TOO young to start thinking about fashion and beauty – if you want a flat forehead, tiny feet or a neck like a giraffe. Children's bones are so flexible that, by binding and pressing, parents have literally squeezed their children into the shapes they wanted.

The aim of this body-bending was to make children more beautiful. The families that did it lived mostly in times or places where ideas of beauty were very different from our own. What now seems cruel was normal in 18th century China or America.

Small is beautiful

Wealthy Chinese people began tightly bandaging the feet of their infant daughters more than 1,000 years ago. As the girls grew up, the bindings broke their toes and deformed their feet, causing terrible pain. Binding a girl's feet showed how well off her family was: she was crippled, so she could neither walk nor work.

◄ **Small slippers**
Women with bound feet slipped them into unbelievably small shoes: some measuring just 10 cm (4 in) from heel to toe. As walking was almost impossible, the shoes got very little wear and were made of fine materials – the set shown here are silk. Foot-binding in China ended in 1911 after the country's revolution gave women more rights and freedom.

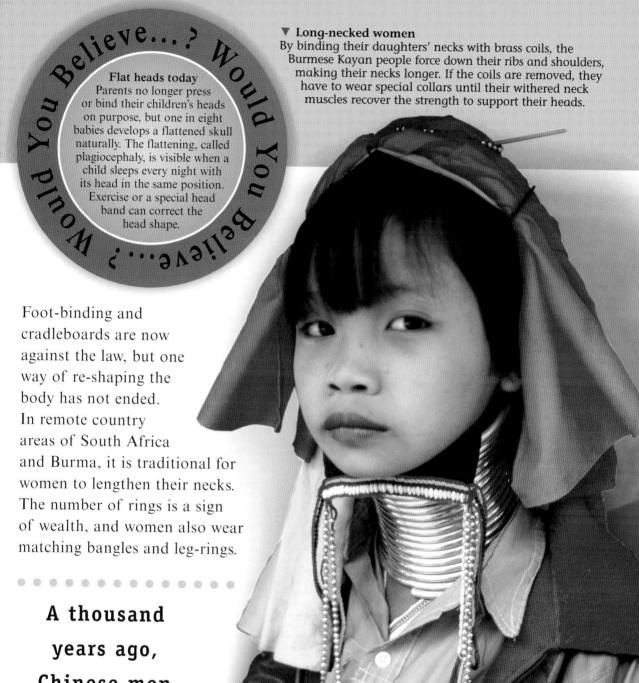

Would You Believe...? Would You Believe...? Would You Believe...?

Flat heads today
Parents no longer press or bind their children's heads on purpose, but one in eight babies develops a flattened skull naturally. The flattening, called plagiocephaly, is visible when a child sleeps every night with its head in the same position. Exercise or a special head band can correct the head shape.

▼ **Long-necked women**
By binding their daughters' necks with brass coils, the Burmese Kayan people force down their ribs and shoulders, making their necks longer. If the coils are removed, they have to wear special collars until their withered neck muscles recover the strength to support their heads.

Foot-binding and cradleboards are now against the law, but one way of re-shaping the body has not ended. In remote country areas of South Africa and Burma, it is traditional for women to lengthen their necks. The number of rings is a sign of wealth, and women also wear matching bangles and leg-rings.

A thousand years ago, Chinese men would not marry a woman if her feet had not been bound

SMOOTH, BLANK AND seamless, human skin is like an artist's canvas. No wonder some of us can't resist decorating it. Skin renews itself regularly, so marks on it soon fade. The only way to make them permanent is by tattooing (injecting dye under the skin) or by cutting to make scars.

Skin art is ancient, but faded from use in Europe as Christianity spread. Some Christians believed that their holy book, the Bible, forbade marking the skin. Tattooing continued in other parts of the world, especially around the Pacific Ocean.

Would You Believe...? Would You Believe...?

Tattoos and medicine
In many parts of the world, tattooing was a traditional way of protecting against disease. Samoan people believed that tattoos stopped them getting rheumatism. But tattoos do not stop disease, and may even spread it if the needles used to inject the dye are not perfectly clean.

◀ **Maori faces**
Among the native Maori people of New Zealand, a man without tattoos on his face was once thought of as someone of no importance. The elaborate patterns were originally painfully applied with a sharp bone chisel. Dipping the chisel into soot made the swirling marks permanent.

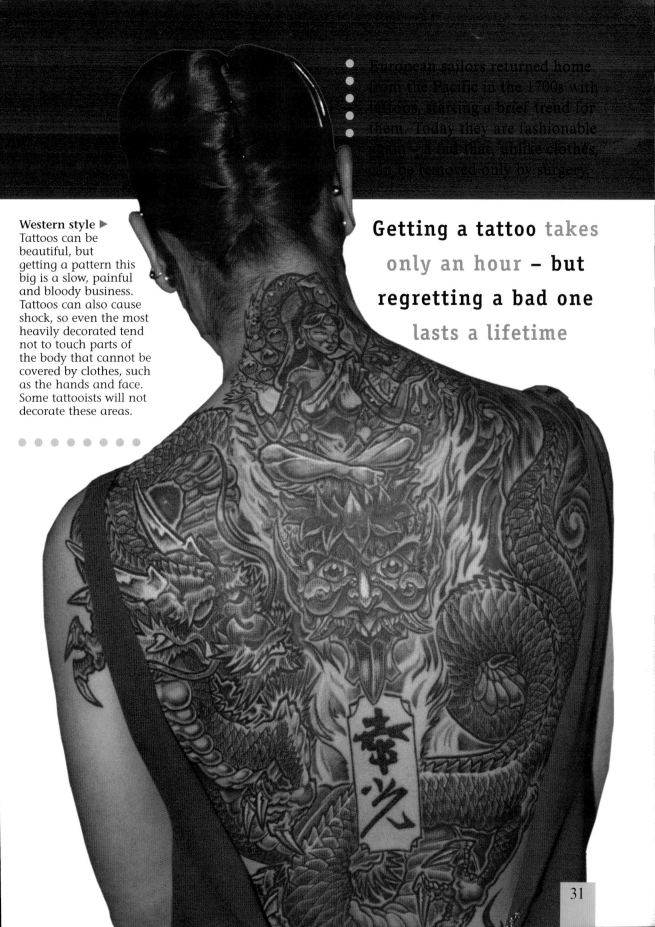

Western style ▶
Tattoos can be beautiful, but getting a pattern this big is a slow, painful and bloody business. Tattoos can also cause shock, so even the most heavily decorated tend not to touch parts of the body that cannot be covered by clothes, such as the hands and face. Some tattooists will not decorate these areas.

Getting a tattoo takes only an hour – but regretting a bad one lasts a lifetime

My Feet are Killing Me

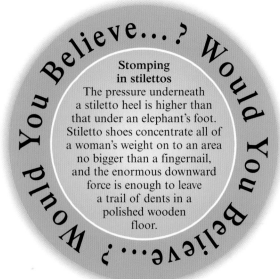

DANCING, WALKING, jogging or just posing, a beautiful shoe shouts, "I've got style!" For centuries, the fashionable have splashed out on their feet, paying cobblers to make colourful and sometimes crazy footwear. At times, the styles have been so extreme that those who wore them couldn't walk.

Poulaines ▶
These shoes from the 15th century got their name, poulaines, from the French word for Poland – where they were first made. As fashions changed, the pointed toes grew longer and longer, until they were twice the length of the feet inside them.

◀ Chopines
Chopines were a type of shoe with a towering sole, fashionable during the 16th and 17th centuries. They were particularly popular in Italy: women in the city of Venice wore chopines 75 cm (2.5 ft) high. This Venetian example is made of silk, wood and leather.

These deliberately useless shoes showed that the owner was rich and never needed to walk more than a few steps. The shoes of poorer people were usually practical, comfortable and watertight because they were always on their feet working.

Would You Believe...?

Stomping in stilettos
The pressure underneath a stiletto heel is higher than that under an elephant's foot. Stiletto shoes concentrate all of a woman's weight on to an area no bigger than a fingernail, and the enormous downward force is enough to leave a trail of dents in a polished wooden floor.

Pointy toes ▼
Shoes with pointed toes were first fashionable in the late 11th century. For a long time, the tip was shaped to look like the horn of a ram or the tail of a scorpion.

High heels were invented in Persia to keep feet out of the burning desert sand

Today, fashions in shoes change quickly, but surprisingly few styles are really new. Platform soles and pointy toes are centuries old. Only the stiletto has a short history – it was invented in Italy in the 1950s.

▲ Pattens
Shoe styles from the past were at their swankiest when the streets were muddiest. The way to keep expensive silk and velvet shoes clean was to slip them into pattens. These extra soles lifted your feet clear of the filth.

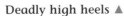

Deadly high heels ▲
Tall, narrow and dangerously pointed, stiletto heels were named after the thick-bladed daggers once used by Italian assassins. Though they make the leg look longer, they also make walking difficult and uncomfortable.

33

The Unkindest
Cut of All

THE FIRST PEOPLE to benefit from modern plastic surgery were not vain men and women, but injured soldiers. Blasted by shells and bombs in World War I (1914–1918), they had their shattered faces reconstructed by patient surgeons and dentists.

Wartime experience gave surgeons new skills. In the USA, a few began to use them to improve angular noses and remove wrinkles with "face lifts". Breast reduction began in the 1920s, but enlargement was not routine until the 1960s.

Would You Believe...?

Where'd by dose go?
Early cosmetic surgeons padded out faces with some strange substances, including goose grease, white oak bark and Vaseline. But the favourite was candle wax. Unfortunately it softened in the sun, and patients found that their costly nose jobs melted on the beach.

◀ **The first nose-job**
Plastic surgery started in India some 2,000 years ago with the first nose-jobs. Removal of the nose was a punishment for crimes such as stealing. Surgeons rebuilt it with a leaf-shaped patch of skin cut from the forehead. Flipped and lowered, it grew into a new nose. Wooden breathing tubes kept the nostrils open.

Changing faces ▲
Cosmetic surgeons today can change the appearance of the face – and even make a man look like a woman. British celebrity Pete Burns had a nose-job and collagen (animal protein) injections to model himself a face (main picture) that he believed better fitted his personality.

Obsession with youth and beauty has made cosmetic surgery big business. But many of the operations carried out are unnecessary, and some of the clinics that perform minor treatments use untrained staff. Patients whose operations are botched need costly corrective treatment.

Not the knife

For a few, cosmetic surgery is essential. But for most of us, exercise, less sun and stress and a healthier diet are safer, cheaper ways to improve our appearance.

One 15th-century German surgeon could "make a new nose if it has been lopped off and the dogs have eaten it"

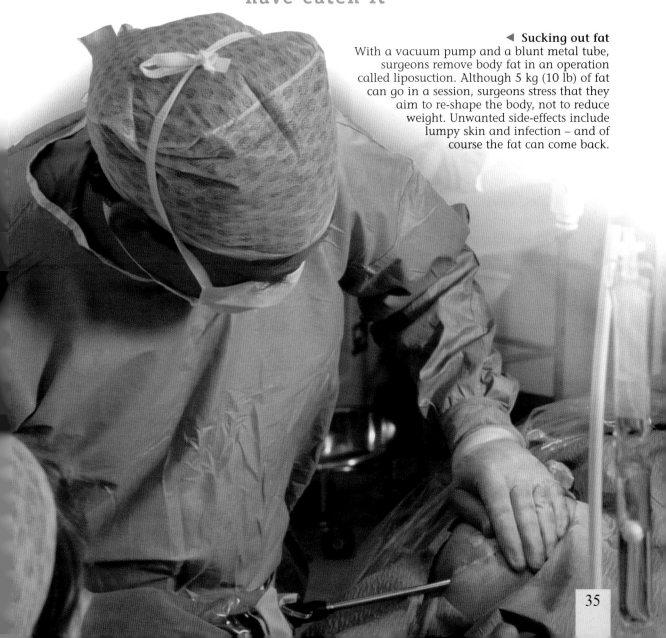

◀ **Sucking out fat**
With a vacuum pump and a blunt metal tube, surgeons remove body fat in an operation called liposuction. Although 5 kg (10 lb) of fat can go in a session, surgeons stress that they aim to re-shape the body, not to reduce weight. Unwanted side-effects include lumpy skin and infection – and of course the fat can come back.

Why Stop at the Ear?

PROUDLY PIERCED punks may not know it, but their punctured lips, noses, ears, brows and tongues celebrate a form of body decoration that is older than history. Nose-rings are mentioned in the Bible, and some mummies from ancient Egypt have pierced ears.

Ear-piercing has always been popular for women, but in Europe and the USA few men wore earrings until the hippie era of the 1960s. Body piercing began in the American homosexual community some ten years later, and the trend spread.

● ● ● ● ● ● ● ● ● ● ● ● ● ● ● ●

◀ **Lip plates**
To make themselves more beautiful, Mursi women of southwest Ethiopia insert clay plates into cuts made in their lower lips. Gradually increasing the size of plate stretches the piercing to the diameter of a saucer. Many also stretch their ear-lobes with plugs in a similar way.

Radical or safe?

The risk of infection from a botched piercing is real, so don't try piercing even an ear-lobe at home. Avoid cheap jewellery and follow hygiene instructions carefully to avoid infection and speed up the healing of the hole.

King of the rings ▶

Cuban Luis Antonio Aguero claims to be the most pierced man in the world. Here, he is wearing 175 pieces of jewellery. Since this picture was taken, he has doubled the number of holes in his head.

Would You Believe...?

Pierced pirates

For a swashbuckling pirate, a gold hoop earring is essential – or is it? Piercing for men was fashionable in the 1500s, but they wore pearls and jewels in their ears, not hoops. And fashion conscious men of the 18th century – pirates included – would never dream of wearing earrings.

The Karankawa Indians of the Texas coast wore small pieces of cane through their pierced nipples

◀ **Aztec lip plug**

An Aztec nobleman would have worn this plug through his pierced lower lip in about 1500. At about 6 cm (2.5 in) long, this lip plug is as big as some of the most extreme lip ornaments of today. The shaft is made from rock crystal, and the ends are gold.

All My Own Teeth

Would You Believe...? Would You Believe...? Would You Believe...?

Crooked dentists
Until laws were introduced requiring dentists to be trained, anybody could pull teeth and fit dentures. The worst dentists wouldn't let patients go home without an extraction. By pulling a front tooth, they made sure that the patient would quickly return to buy a costly false tooth.

AT FASHIONABLE parties in the past there was little laughter. The jokes were funny enough, but guests kept their lips shut to hide their rotten teeth. Dental care improved in the 20th century, but only the rich could afford it. Just 40 years ago, four out of five older people had no teeth of their own.

The famous and fashionable hid their gaps with dentures (false teeth). Until about 1790, when porcelain dentures became popular, dentists carved them from bone or ivory, or took teeth from animals or from the dead.

Buying teeth
Wealthy people of the late 18th century found an alternative to dentures. Their dentists pulled out their bad teeth and pushed healthy teeth bought from poor children into the holes. These "live tooth transplants" lasted ten years.

First falsies ▶

In the 7th century BCE, the Etruscan people of Italy filled gaps using extracted teeth. They fixed them to gold bands that slipped over the remaining teeth. Nobody thought of a better way of holding teeth in place for another 2,500 years.

The fashion in 9th century Mayan Mexico was to decorate front teeth with jade and turquoise stones

◀ **Porcelain smile**
French dentist Nicolas Dubois de Chémant was the first to make successful porcelain teeth. This cartoon from 1798 shows a potential patient admiring a porcelain smile.

▼ **Famous teeth**
In 16th century England false teeth were rare, so Queen Elizabeth I packed her mouth with cloth to fill out her sunken face. American president George Washington was not much luckier. His elk and human dentures were held together with powerful springs.

For those needing more than one or two teeth, wars provided a wonderful opportunity. When great battles ended, scavengers with pliers moved among the dead (and nearly dead) pulling teeth to sell. After the 1815 battle of Waterloo, London's rich wore "Waterloo teeth".

▲ **Washington kept his mouth shut to hide his dentures.**

Hippo teeth ▶
Ivory (the tusks of elephants and the teeth of hippopotamuses) supplied the raw materials for countless expensive sets of dentures. The plates and back teeth of this pair are carved from hippo ivory; the front teeth are human.

Makeup and Beauty

◀ **Greek rouge**
To redden their cheeks, ancient Greek women used the roots of alkanet – a plant of the forget-me-not family. Its red colour contrasted with the white powder used elsewhere on their faces.

P AINTED WITH rouge and eye-liner, a beautiful face gazes at us with confidence. Apart from her hat, this woman could be a catwalk model, but she is from the 12th century BCE. As an Egyptian queen, her makeup would have been prepared by a slave-girl.

Over the following centuries, there has rarely been a time when women, and sometimes men, too, have not coloured their faces for beauty – or to disguise their age.

◀ **Palace chic**
In this portrait sculpture, Queen Nefertiti's eyes are outlined with kohl (see page 42), and her eyebrows are painted. She is not, however, wearing the blue or green eyeshadow that was popular with Egyptian women.

▲ **Egyptian palette**
The ancient Egyptian name for makeup palettes like this one sounded the same as their word for "protect". Copper minerals used in some Egyptian eye makeup helped to prevent eye disease.

From Egyptian eyeliner to lipstick from Ur (now in Iraq), most makeup has ancient origins. Women relied on cosmetics made at home or by hairdressers and pharmacists until they were first mass-produced during the 20th century.

Egyptian workmen went on strike in 1158 BCE because they ran out of eye makeup

◀ **Beautiful blokes**
In the late 17th century, European men were as painted as their wives. They powdered their faces, then applied rouge and lipstick. Velvet or silk hearts, stars or moons, known as "beauty patches", completed the look.

Cult cosmetics ▶
Makeup doesn't have to make the wearer look younger or more beautiful. Shock-rocker Marilyn Manson uses radical cosmetics to emphasise his already dramatic features. The result is calculated to charm his fans – and terrify their parents.

MAKEUP TO DIE FOR

sounds like a modern advertising slogan but, until laws controlled cosmetic safety, it was the truth. Many kinds of makeup contained poisons that, at best, blistered your skin. At worst, they killed you.

White face powders were among the most dangerous. The main ingredient of ceruse – the powder that every fashionable 14th century lady wore – was poisonous lead. To redden their cheeks, wealthy men and women commonly used vermilion. This fabulously expensive colour contained mercury – another poison.

Would You Believe...?

Murderous makeup
17th century Italian Tofana di Adamo sold a face-whitening makeup called *Aqua tofana* to other women. When 600 husbands died, Tofana was arrested. She confessed that the makeup contained deadly arsenic. Her customers used it to poison their husbands and inherit their money.

▲ **Deadly nightshade**
The Latin name for the deadly nightshade plant is *belladonna*, meaning "beautiful lady". This name comes from its use – drops of the plant oil make the pupil of the eye bigger and more attractive. The plant's English name reveals its other quality – if swallowed, it kills.

Kohl eyeliner ▶
This 3,300-year-old glass tube from Egypt once held kohl eyeliner, which was made from antimony. Small doses of this metallic element can cause headaches, dizziness and depression. Larger doses are deadly.

16th century women
used oil of vitriol
(sulphuric acid)
as a skin cleanser

▲ Pale and interesting
The white ceruse powder that England's Queen
Elizabeth I used to paint her face scarred her
skin. To hide the marks, she applied ever-thicker
layers. By the time she died, Elizabeth's face
looked like a white mask.

Poisons in clothes

Fashionable clothes and shoes
have never been as toxic
as makeup, but the people
who make them have often
suffered. Hatters, for
instance, died of mercury
poisoning, and the lives of
leather workers were made
shorter by the chemicals
they used in tanning
(treating animal
skins to convert
them to leather).

Most cosmetics today are safe, but
there are still dangerous levels of
mercury in some skin-lightening
products. And a few labels hide
dirty secrets: certain expensive
anti-ageing creams are
made from the tissue
of pregnant women.

Mad as a hatter ▶
The Mad Hatter in Lewis Carroll's
Alice's Adventures in Wonderland
was driven mad by his job. Hatters
used mercury to roughen the fibres
of felt hats. It slowly poisoned
them, causing twitching
limbs, confused speech,
mental illness and death.

*In this
Style
10/6*

What's so Weird about That?

OUTRAGEOUS, DARING, extravagant – and sometimes even dangerous – fashion makes our world brighter and our lives livelier. Although we gasp at daring catwalk styles, a glance through this book shows that, in a different time or place, someone has almost always dressed in an even more amazing way.

These styles from different cultures and ages make fashion more interesting and varied. You may not want to wear a towering wig, but the world would be a duller place if nobody ever had.

Would You Believe…? Would You Believe…?

Selling dreams
Most top fashion models are a size 8 or smaller, but about half of all women in the UK take a size 16. No wonder it's so hard to find new clothes that suit you! The fashion industry may be selling a glamorous dream, but it is so far from reality that buying clothes can be misery.

◄ **The catwalk**
Catwalk models show off styles that only the very wealthiest can buy. Through *haute couture* (high fashion) like this, a few top designers control the clothes millions of us wear – whether we like it or not.

Fashion slaves
Fashion may seem like fun but, as you've seen, it can be ridiculous and harmful, too. Looking just the same as everyone else may be reassuring, but it is also expensive and wasteful. Why should this summer's colours, fabrics and styles be different from last summer's?

Don't be afraid to escape from the herd: be yourself, and wear something completely different

Find out More

You can learn more about costume and fashion by checking out these websites and places to visit.

Websites

Costume drama game
http://www.museumofcostume.co.uk/
htmlContent/game.htm
Test your knowledge of fashion from four eras.

Design a textile
http://www.vam.ac.uk/vastatic/microsites/
british_galleries/designa/textile/textile.html
Mix and match colours and patterns, then print out your fabric sample.

Fashion era
http://www.fashion-era.com
The place to look for hard facts about fashion.

Kimonos
http://web-japan.org/kidsweb/virtual/
kimono/top.html
Find out about traditional Japanese costume, and create your own kimono.

Corsets
http://www.vam.ac.uk/collections/fashion/
corset/index.html
Discover the secret history of corsets and crinolines with this Victoria & Albert Museum virtual exhibit.

Henna tattoos
http://www.mehendiworld.com
The story of *mehendi* (henna tattoos), with practical instructions and designs to copy.

All about shoes
http://www.allaboutshoes.ca/en
Learn about high heels and more on this website.

History of sneakers
http://www.sneakerhead.com/
sneaker-history-p1.html
All you need to know about sneakers and trainers.

Places to visit

The Victoria & Albert Museum
Cromwell Road
London SW7 2RL
Telephone: 020 7942 2000
Website: http://www.vam.ac.uk/collections/
index.html
This vast museum in London is a treasure trove for fashion fans, with beautifully displayed original costumes from the past, and constantly changing special exhibitions. The V&A is not just fashion: its collection includes examples from many other kinds of art, design and craft.

Bath Museum of Costume
Bennett Street
Bath BA1 2QH
Telephone: 01225 477 173
Website: http://www.museumofcostume.co.uk
Displays at this museum in the centre of Bath illustrate changing styles of dress over the last 400 years. There are regular themed shows, and the permanent exhibition is divided into three sections: fashion before 1800; 19th century clothes; and costume since 1900.

Shambellie House Museum of Costume
New Abbey
Dumfriesshire DG2 8HQ
Telephone: 01387 850 375
Website: http://www.nms.ac.uk/costume/
home/index.asp
In this Victorian house near Dumfries, the main rooms are shown as if frozen in time, displaying costumes from seven periods between 1882 and 1952.

Manchester Gallery of Costume
Platt Hall
Rusholme
Manchester M14 5LL
Telephone: 0161 224 5217
Website: http://www.manchestergalleries.org/
html/costume/goc_home.jsp
One of the largest collections of costumes and accessories in Britain. Unusually, the gallery shows not only high fashion, but also the clothes of ordinary working people.

Glossary

Did you read anything you didn't understand? Some of the more complicated and unusual terms used in this book are explained here.

armour
Protective clothing worn in battle to prevent injuries.

arsenic
Poisonous metal-like chemical: one-twentieth of a teaspoonful would kill an adult.

boycott
Way of protesting by not buying or using a product or service.

catwalk
Long, raised stage along which models walk in fashion shows.

cobbler
Worker who makes or repairs shoes.

dandy
Elegantly dressed man who takes great care about his appearance.

denture
Artificial teeth, and the plate or frame that holds them in place.

embroidery
Decorative, colourful pattern of stitches on a garment.

extinction
Killing or death of the world's very last plant or animal of a particular kind.

flapper
Woman from the 1920s who did not obey traditional rules of dress and behaviour.

geisha
Traditional female Japanese performer, and paid entertainer of men.

knight
Armoured warrior of the 12th–16th centuries.

Maori
Native people of New Zealand.

mercury
Poisonous, shiny, silver-coloured liquid metal.

Mohican
Hairstyle in which the scalp is shaved, apart from a narrow central strip.

pharmacist
Worker who makes or supplies healing drugs.

plastic surgery
Surgery to change the body or face, either to correct deformed or damaged features (reconstructive surgery), or to make the patient look prettier (cosmetic surgery).

porcelain
Fragile, glassy type of fine-quality pottery.

punk
Freedom movement that began in the 1970s, with its own distinctive, outrageous styles of dress, dance and music.

revolution
When many people rise up to take power away from an unpopular government.

silk
Fine, smooth fabric made from threads spun by a moth.

stiletto
Long, slim knife, and the high shoe heel named after it.

surgeon
Doctor trained in surgery (cutting open the human body).

tailor
Worker who makes or adjusts clothes.

tanning
Treatment of animal skins to make them into soft, bendy leather.

tattoo
Permanent pattern on the skin, made by rubbing or injecting colouring materials into tiny pricks or cuts.

tiara
Small, jewelled, woman's crown, now usually worn only by queens or brides.

uniform
Matching clothing worn to show authority or membership of a group, especially military or official groups such as armies and police forces.

witchcraft
The practice of secret, magic actions, usually aiming to change or foresee future events.

Index

Picture credits

The publisher would like to thank the following for their kind permission to reproduce their photographs:

Position key: c=centre; b=bottom; l=left; r=right; t=top

Cover: Front: tr: Dynamic Graphics Group/Creatas/Alamy; cr: Getty Images/Chip Simons; bl: Mary Evans Picture Library/Alamy; tl: Getty Images/Kenny Johnson. Background: OUP/Photodisc.

4c: R Sheridan/Ancient Art & Architecture Collection Ltd; 5l: Sunset Boulevard/Corbis; 5r: Doug Peters/allactiondigital/Empics; 6r: Brooklyn Museum of Art/Corbis; 7l: Gianni Dagli Orti/Corbis; 8l: Araldo de Luca/Corbis; 9bc: Museum of London/Heritage Image Partnership; 10r: Museum of London/Heritage Image Partnership; 10bl: Darren Sawyer; 11b: Historical Picture Archive/Corbis; 11tl: Akg-Images/Erich Lessing; 11l: Akg-Images/Erich Lessing; 11cl: Akg-Images/Erich Lessing; 12r: Araldo de Luca/Corbis; 13b: Hulton-Deutsch Collection/Corbis; 14l: Mary Evans Picture Library; 15r: 20th Century Fox/The Kobal Collection; 16br: Michael Malsan Historic Photographs/Corbis; 16l: Museum of London/Heritage Image Partnership; 17r: Adrianna Williams/ Zefa/Corbis; 19bl: Museum of London/Heritage Image Partnership; 19r: Tim Graham/Corbis; 20r: Conde Nast Archive/Corbis; 21c: Darren Sawyer; 21c: Roderick Eime-Monolith; 22l: Mary Evans Picture Library; 23r: Matthew Mendelsohn/Corbis; 23cl: Darren Sawyer; 24r: Museum of London/Heritage Image Partnership; 25tl: Hulton-Deutsch Collection/Corbis; 26l: Museum of London/Heritage Image Partnership; 27t: Museum of London/Heritage Image Partnership; 27br: Akg-Images; 28bc: Science Museum/Science and Society Picture Library; 28cr: Lake County Museum/Corbis; 29r: Daniel Laine/Corbis; 30cr: Wellcome Trust; 31c: Gene Blevins/Corbis; 32cl: V&A; 32t: Museum of London/Heritage Image Partnership; 33bl: V&A; 33br: Saunders Photographic; 34bl: Wellcome Trust; 34c: Steve Jennings/Corbis; 34r: Rune Hellestad/Corbis; 35c: Science Photo Library; 36l: Photo Researchers/Corbis; 36b: Akg-Images/Erich Lessing; 37tr: Hussein Akhtar/Corbis Sygma; 37b: Akg-Images/Erich Lessing; 38r: Science Museum/Science and Society Picture Library; 39t: Science Museum/Science and Society Picture Library; 39b: Science Museum/Science and Society Picture Library; 40cr: DK Limited/Corbis; 40l: Archivo Iconografico, S.A./Corbis; 41br: Hubert Boesl/dpa/Corbis; 42r: The British Museum/Heritage Image Partnership; 43tl: Ann Ronan Picture Library/Heritage Image Partnership; 43br: Lake County Museum/Corbis; 44bl: Stephane Cardinale/People